HAL•LEONARD

BANJO
PLAY-ALONG

VOL. 4

Old-Time Christmas

Recording credits:
Mike Schmidt – Banjo, Guitar, Bass, Autoharp
Bruce King – Mandolin, Guitar

ISBN 978-1-4803-4547-8

HAL•LEONARD®
CORPORATION

7777 W. BLUEMOUND RD. P.O. BOX 13819 MILWAUKEE, WI 53213

In Australia Contact:
Hal Leonard Australia Pty. Ltd.
4 Lentara Court
Cheltenham, Victoria, 3192 Australia
Email: ausadmin@halleonard.com.au

Visit Hal Leonard Online at
www.halleonard.com

Performance Notes
By Mike Schmidt

Thank you for purchasing this book, *Old-Time Christmas.* Please note that these arrangements are for 5-string banjo. While several of the included tunes are in a bluegrass style, there are also those that are not. They are perfectly playable on the 5-string, but they're not bluegrass.

In fact, I can imagine a classical guitar approach on several of them. Some of these are fairly slow, so the cardinal rule of never repeating a right-hand finger without a rest or another note between is broken quite a lot in this collection. Particularly thumbs. You will see a lot of double thumbs. But again, the songs are not so fast as to present a problem.

We should also mention the "feel" of certain songs. Depending on the tempo, you may notice that the picking is steady, giving every note equal time. On other, slower songs, you might feel that they swing a bit, meaning that for every group of two notes, the first is just slightly longer, and the second slightly shorter. "Silent Night" is a good example.

Every tune in this book consists of two banjo parts, or "breaks," with a mandolin break between. The first banjo break is a bit easier and the second approaches an intermediate or advanced level.

Away in a Manger
This one is not too complicated. The main thing to watch is the "strum" symbol that first appears in measure 4, right before Section B. This is not a strum. Instead, it's sort of an arpeggiated chord, but picked. If you've ever seen a harpist's hands when they play a chord, this is similar. I put all fingers down on the strings and then pick them individually, but fairly quickly. It resembles a strum, but with much more control. You'll see this frequently in this collection.

In the backup for the mandolin break, there are a lot of two-finger moves. The second measure of Section D alternates between one fret apart and same fret. Notice the 7-6 at the F, and the 5-5, 3-3, 2-1. Use index and ring for those that are a fret apart (7-6 and 2-1), and middle and ring for the same frets (5-5, 3-3, etc.). This happens more than once in Section D.

13

13

23

In the second measure of Section F (the second banjo break), there's a triplet pattern. (It happens again eight measures later). This is basically three evenly spaced notes in one beat. In this case, the open 1st string is picked with the middle finger, then hammered-on, then pulled off – all in the space of one beat. Listen to the recording to get the feel of it. If it doesn't work, replace the 0-2-0 with a single quarter note 0 on the 1st string.

Hark! The Herald Angels Sing

There's nothing too unusual in the first break until the sixth measure of Section B. There's a 2 to 4 hammer-on on the 3rd string, along with a picked 5th string. I would suggest fretting the 2 with index and hammer with the ring. Notice that the last measure of the first break, immediately before Section C, is a single measure of 2/4.

In the backup, here and in other songs in this book, you will see what may be a break from the banjo prime directive: "If you use the same finger on two notes in a row, without a rest in between, it's wrong!" While this is generally true, it's not etched in stone. These songs are a bit slower, and therefore it's possible to make the exception. The fourth measure of Section D begins with two eighth notes, both picked with thumb. This will happen often here. As mentioned earlier, this is reminiscent of classical guitar style. It isn't lightning fast, so it should be workable.

Aside from those points above, pay attention to the right-hand fingers. The last beat of the second measure of Section F might look like thumb and middle, but it's index and middle.

The last two measures are actual strums. Simply brush with the thumb.

Jingle Bells

This is set in a straightforward Bluegrass style. There isn't a lot of tricky stuff in the first break, but after the A7 to D in Section B, there's a slide on the 3rd string at the G chord (ninth measure of Section B). You're holding down a D chord in the previous measure, so avoid the habit of lifting it up and doing the slide with the middle finger. The index finger is already on the 3rd string 2nd fret, so just do that 2-3 slide with the index.

In the seventh measure of Section E, there are three notes in a row on the 2nd string, picked with index-middle-index. This may be tricky, but it's worth the effort.

Joy to the World

There are definite shortcuts here. In the fifth and sixth measures of Section B, you have a C, followed by a D. Rather than change the chords, just slide the C up two frets to the 3-4 of the D. You're not using any of the lower strings, so it's much smoother this way. The second break is a more melodic one. This is a bit more advanced, but if you're familiar with the basics of melodic banjo, it should be pretty clear.

O Holy Night

We've departed from tradition a bit on this one, a particular favorite of mine. Normally, this tune is in 6/8 and is performed in a somewhat solemn manner. Not here. Instead, it's in cut time and has a definite Bluegrass feel to it. It's a little more upbeat than usual. Have fun with it.

Like others, there are a lot of two-note chord positions in the left hand. The first two measures are a good example. Remember, the chord letters above the staff are for the accompaniment. Just because it says "D," that doesn't mean the banjo needs to put a full D major chord down. Likewise, from Section F to the end of the break, notice that, for the most part, only the 1st and 2nd strings are fretted. There's no need to put the entire chords down. It's much quicker and smoother this way.

In the second break, watch for a few melodic licks. Otherwise, there are no real rough spots.

O Little Town of Bethlehem

The most interesting thing about this one is that I recorded it without picks. I did this for two reasons: 1) it gives the song a softer feel; 2) there are a few arpeggiated chords where I include the ring finger on the right hand. These chords happen in places like the first C chord in Section B, the Dm chord a few measures before Section C, the last C chord on the first page of this tune, and much more frequently in the second banjo break. See the comment about harpist's hands in "Away in a Manger."

The main challenge in this one is that there are some unusual chords – for banjo, anyway.

Silent Night

Because the right hand is holding chord shapes, the main thing to think about is accenting the melody notes within those chords. The first measure of Section B, for example, contains three melody notes; in this case, all are picked with the thumb. There's also a double thumb in that measure. In the first measure of the second page of the song, you will see a measure of A7sus4 followed by A7. The open 5th string is the 7th of the chord, and that's a melody note. So, while it's not difficult to play, the trick is to pull the melody out of the rolls.

The first several measures of the second break use quite a few double thumb rolls. Watch the right hand-finger notation.

We Wish You a Merry Christmas

This is done in fairly quick 3/4 meter, and the banjo is played in a melodic style.

The trickiest part might be the triplet pickup leading into section G. An eighth-note triplet is three notes played evenly on one beat. In this case, the first of the three is picked with the thumb, the second note is hammered-on, the third is picked with the index finger, and then the first note of the next measure is picked with the thumb again. A bit out of the ordinary, it's a nice effect. I'd suggest repeating just those four notes as an exercise. If it doesn't work out, you might consider replacing the triplet with a single G note (3rd string open) on that third beat, like the pickup to Section B.

Away in a Manger

Words by John T. McFarland (v.3)
Music by James R. Murray

G tuning:
(5th-1st) G-D-G-B-D

Key of C

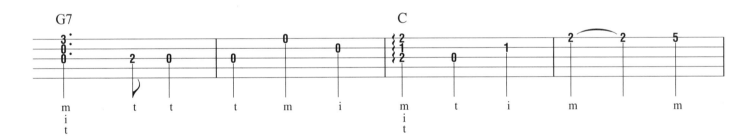

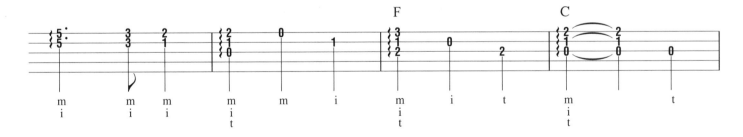

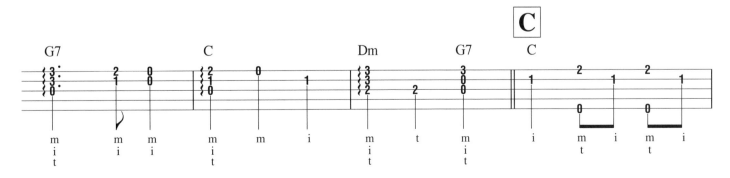

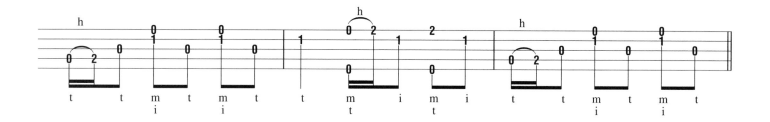

D | Mandolin Break

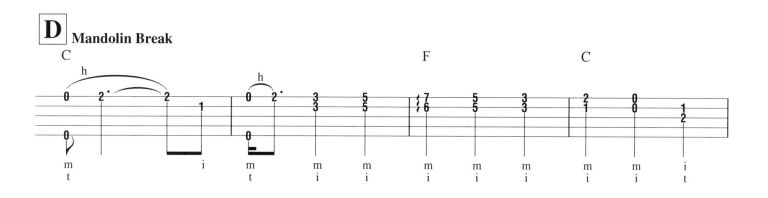

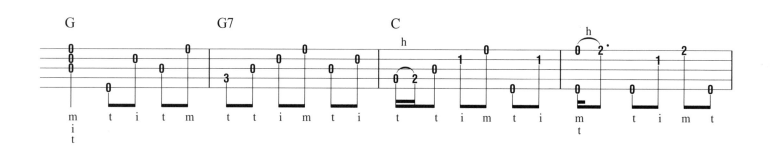

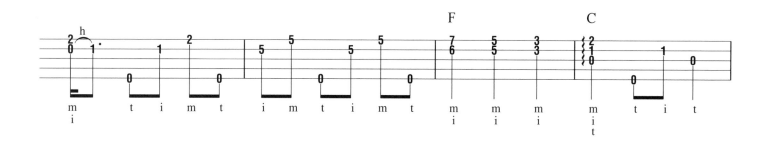

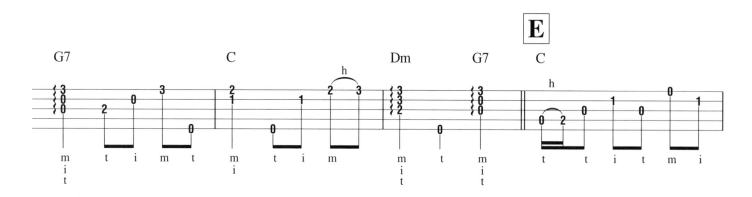

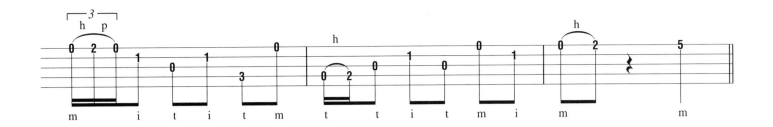

F Banjo Break

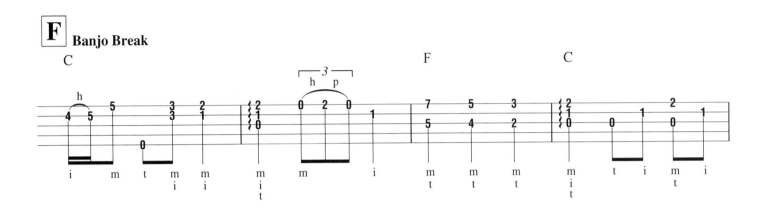

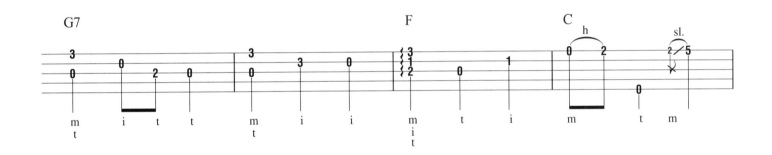

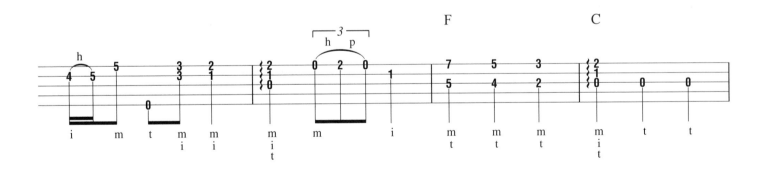

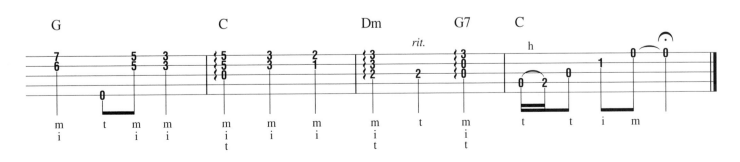

Hark! The Herald Angels Sing

Words by Charles Wesley
Altered by George Whitefield
Music by Felix Mendelssohn-Bartholdy
Arranged by William H. Cummings

G tuning:
(5th-1st) G-D-G-B-D

Key of G

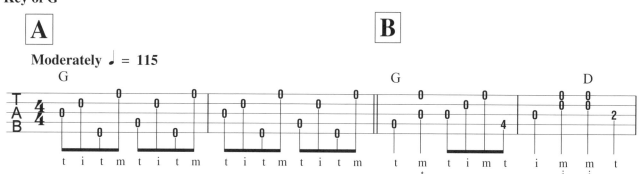

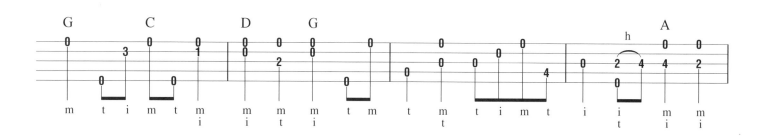

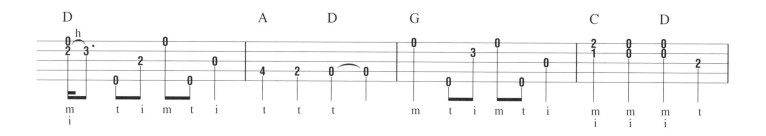

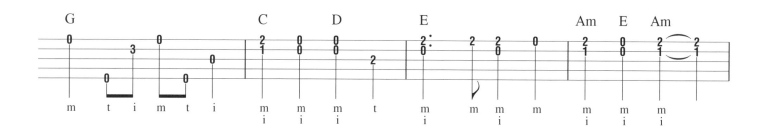

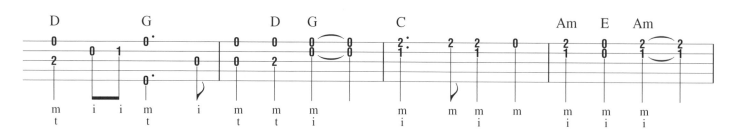

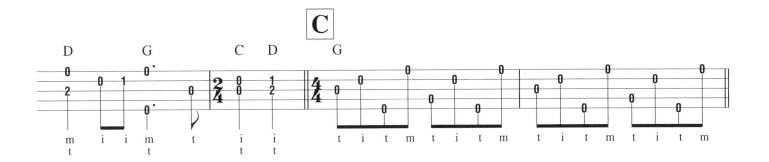

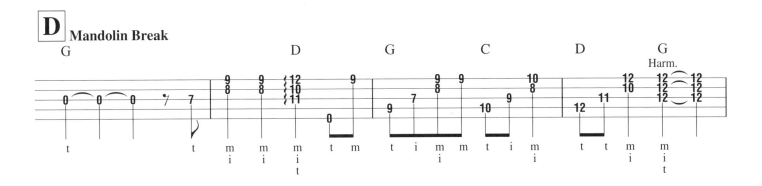

D Mandolin Break

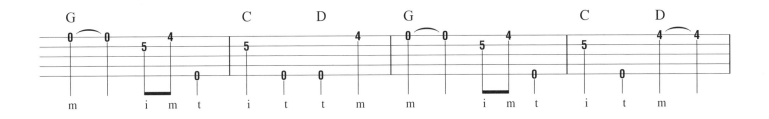

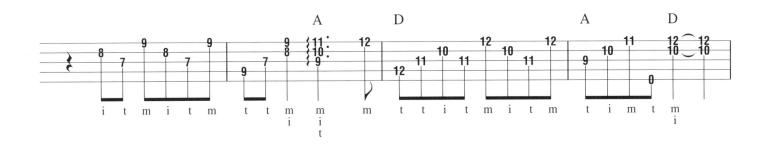

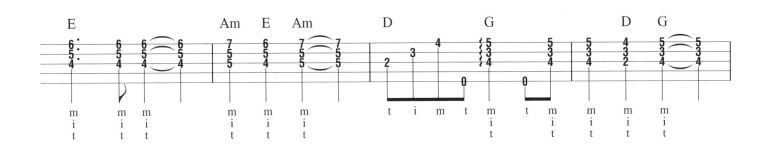

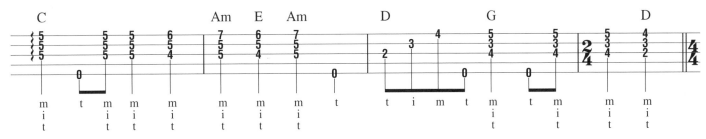

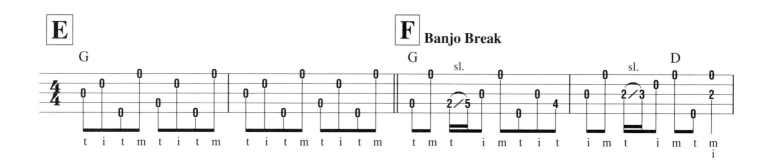

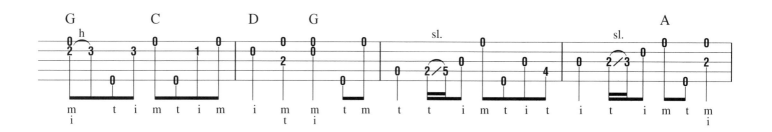

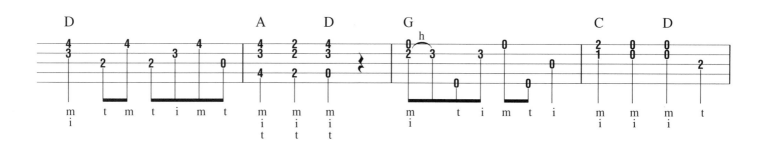

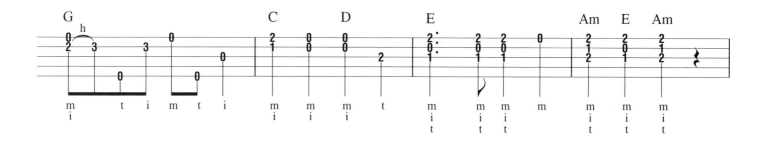

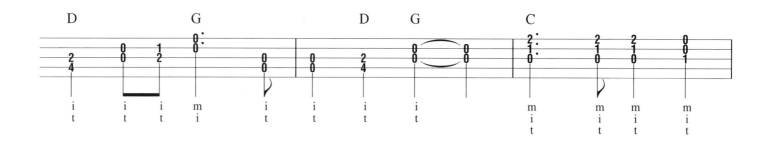

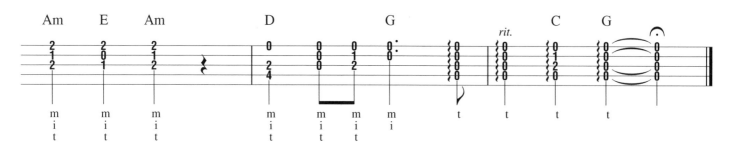

Joy to the World

Words by Isaac Watts
Music by George Frideric Handel
Adapted by Lowell Mason

G tuning:
(5th-1st) G-D-G-B-D

Key of G

Moderately $\quad$ = 88

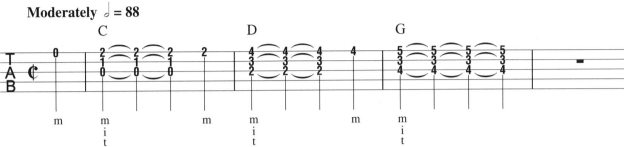

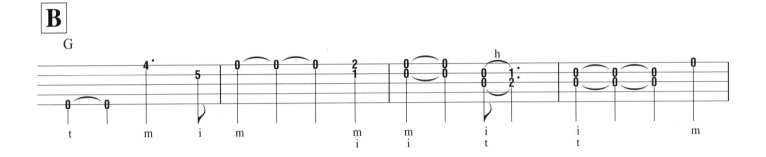

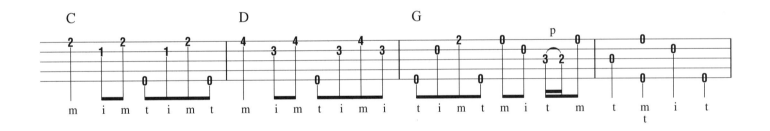

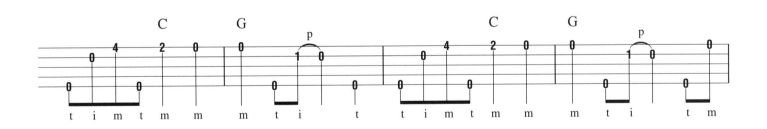

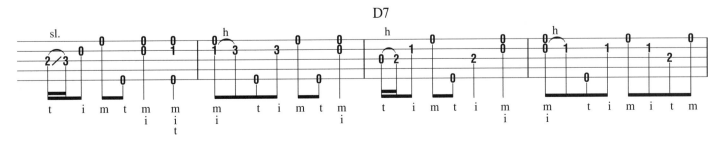

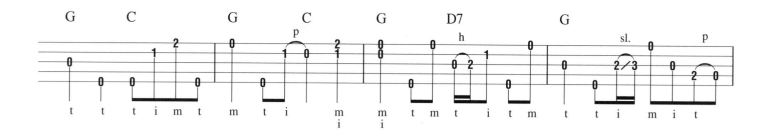

C Mandolin Break

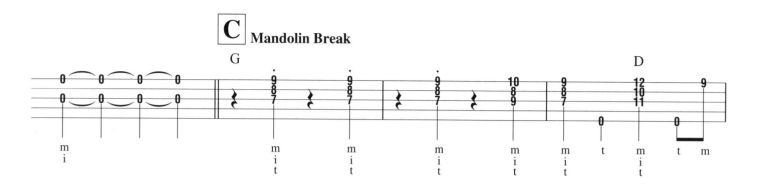

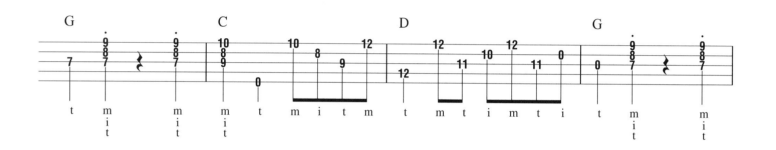

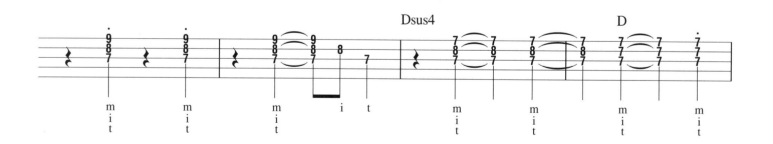

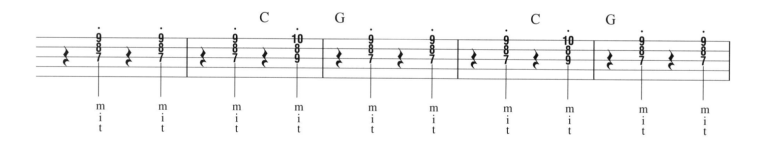

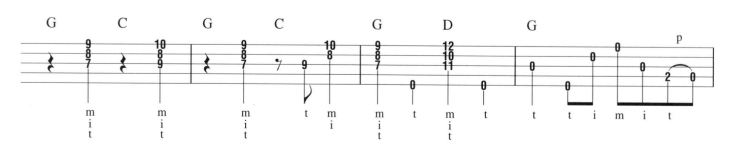

D Banjo Break

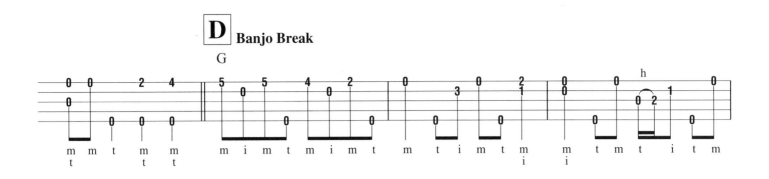

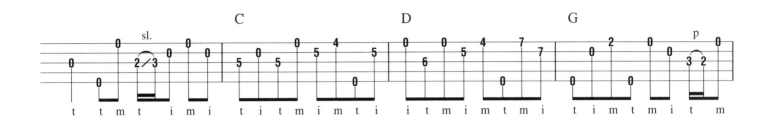

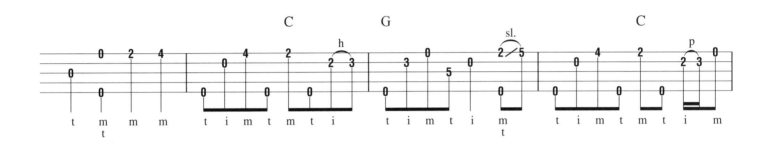

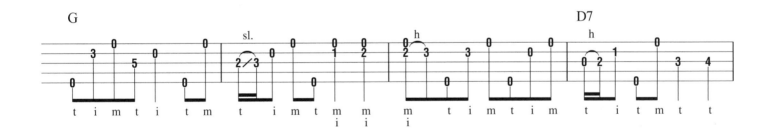

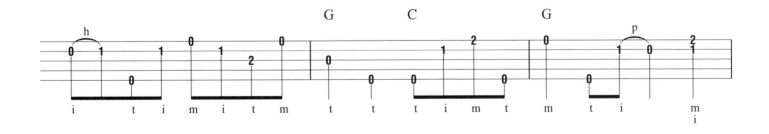

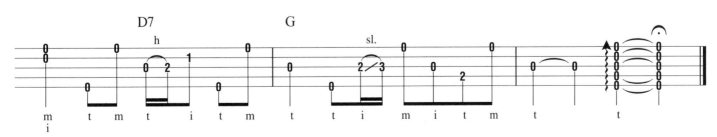

Jingle Bells

Words and Music by J. Pierpont

G tuning:
(5th-1st) G-D-G-B-D

Key of G

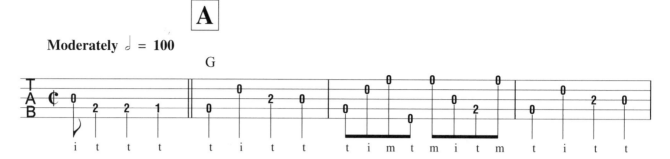

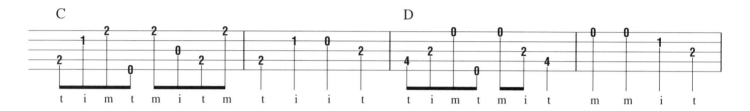

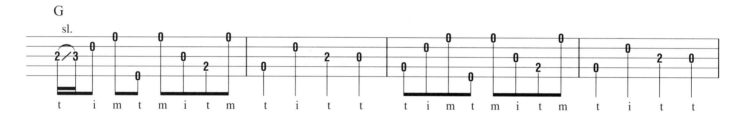

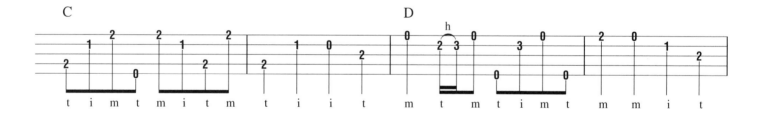

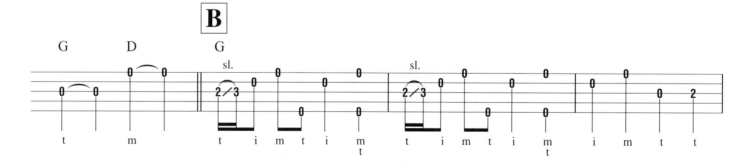

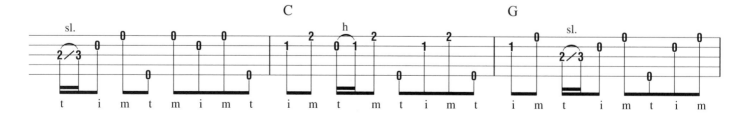

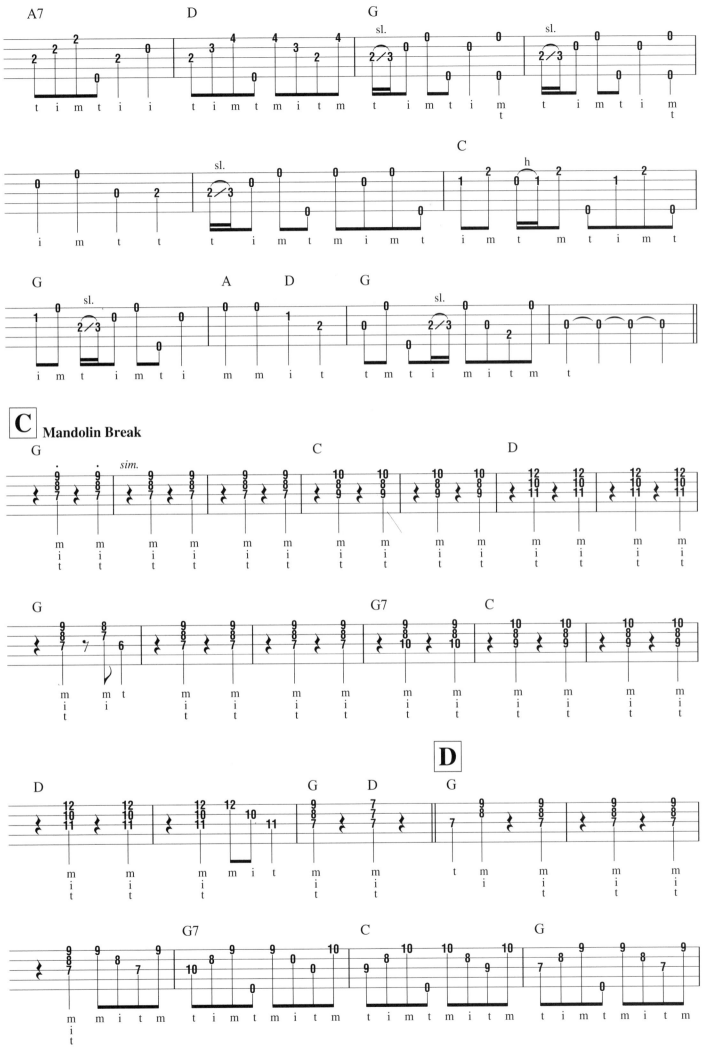

C Mandolin Break

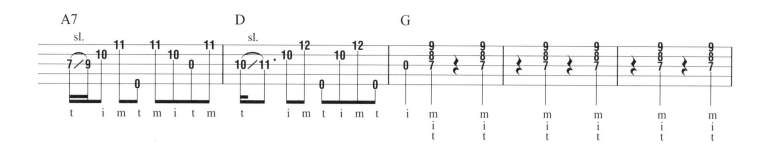

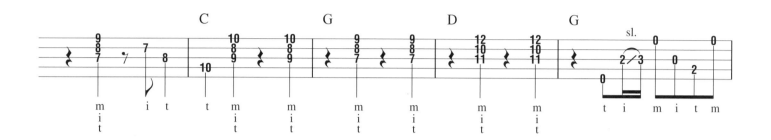

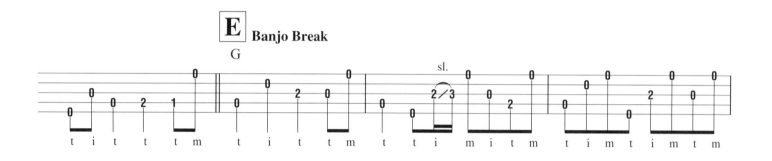

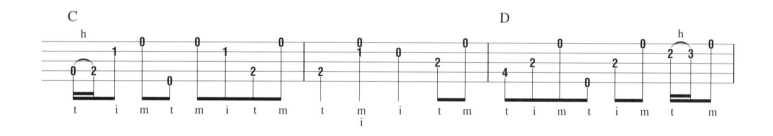

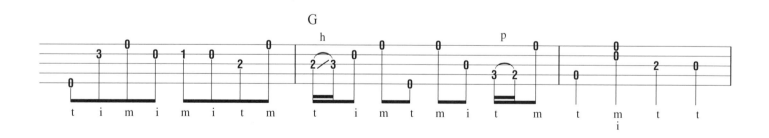

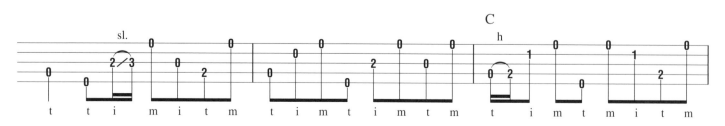

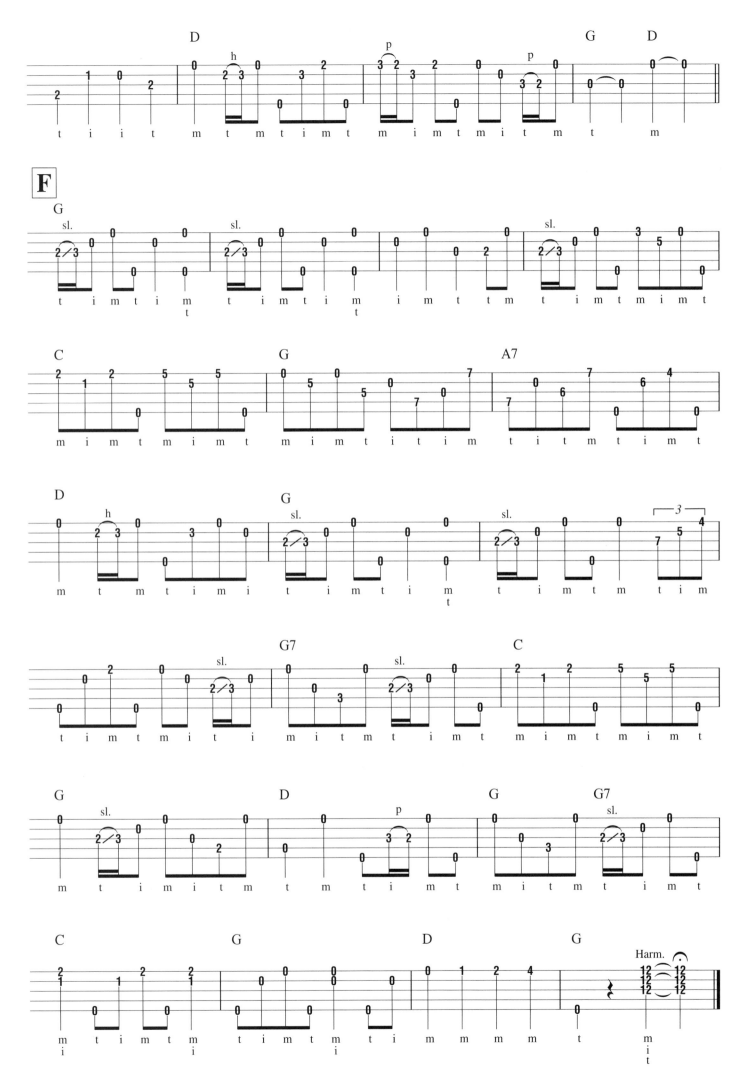

O Holy Night

French Words by Placide Cappeau
English Words by John S. Dwight
Music by Adolphe Adam

G tuning:
(5th-1st) G-D-G-B-D

Key of G

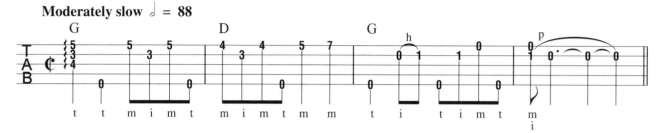

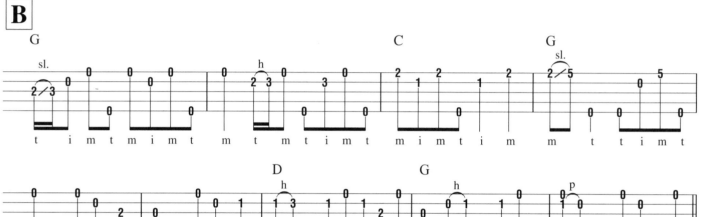

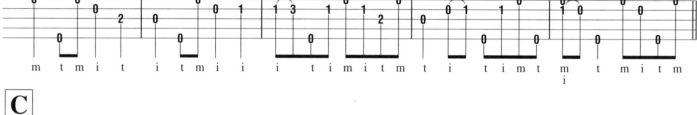

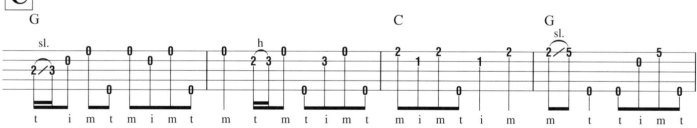

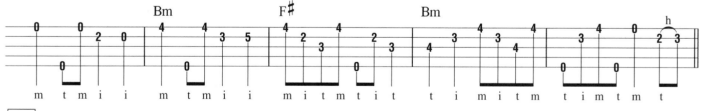

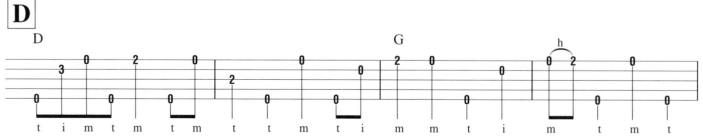

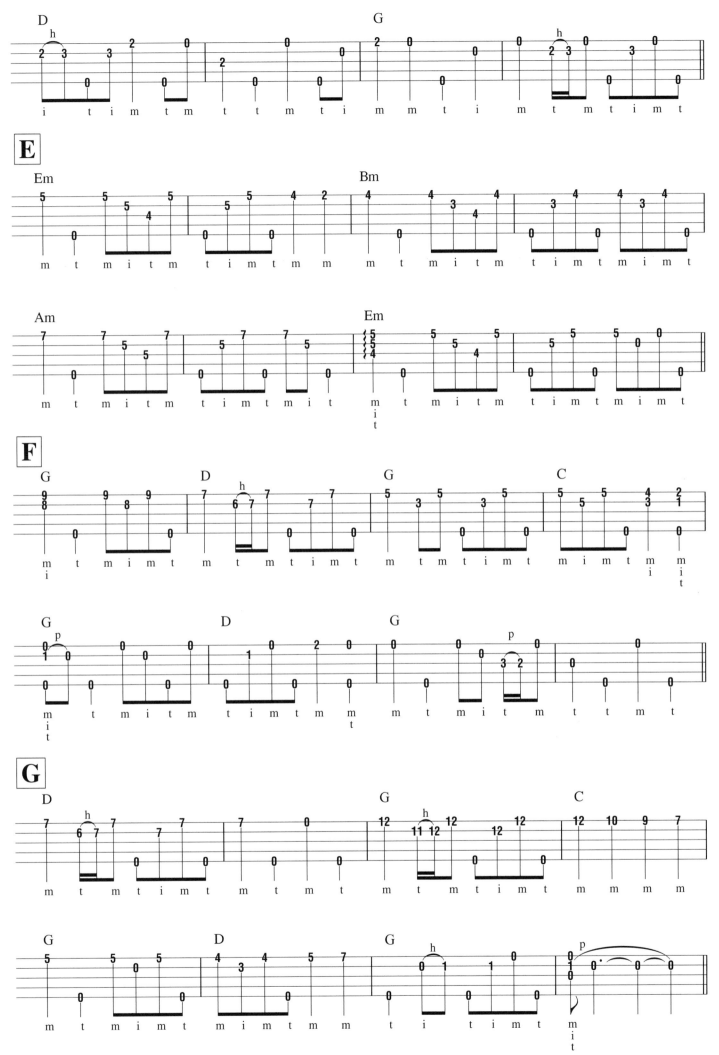

H Mandolin Break

I

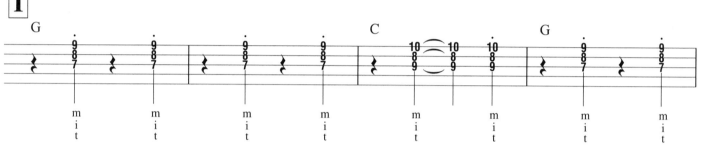

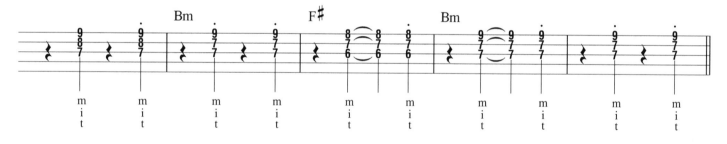

J

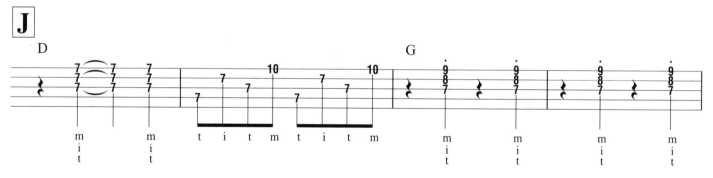

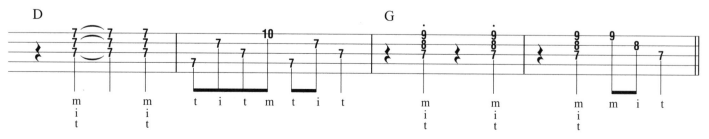

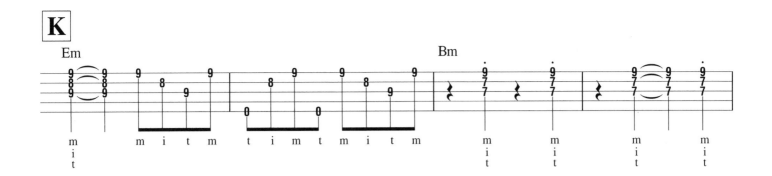

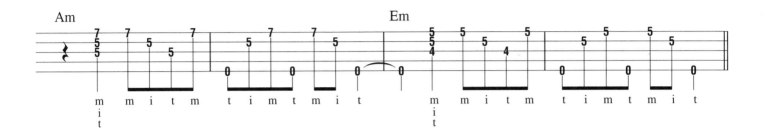

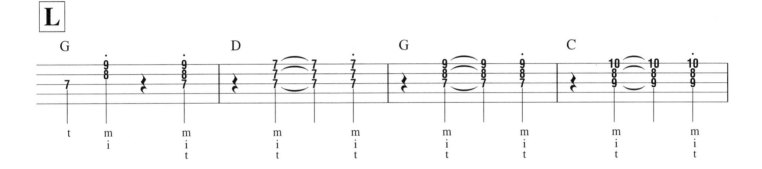

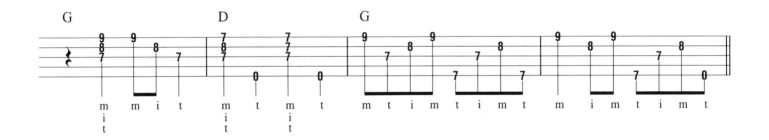

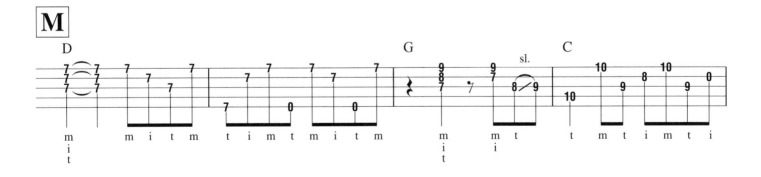

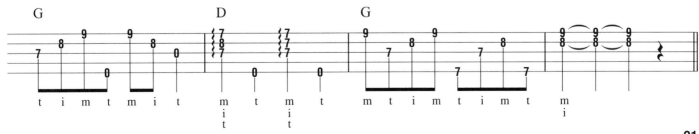

N **Banjo Break**

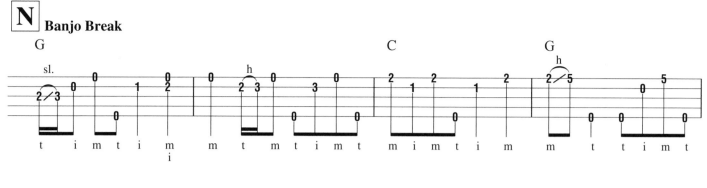

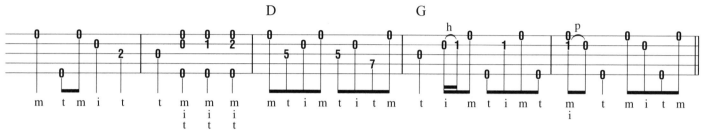

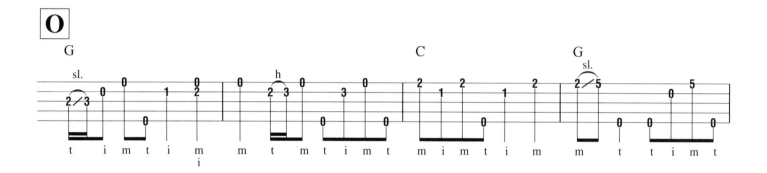

O

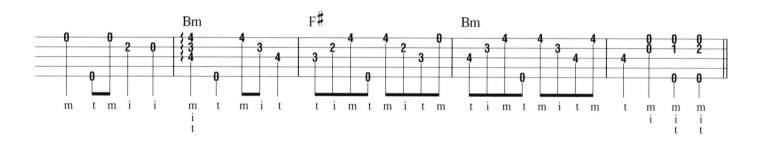

P

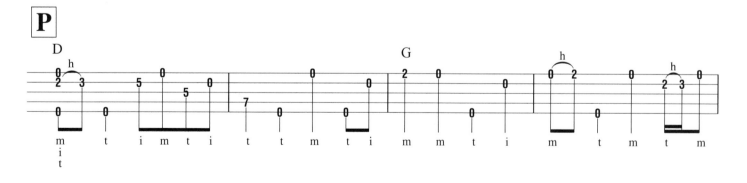

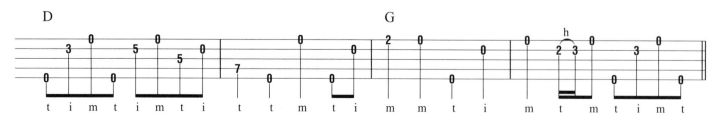

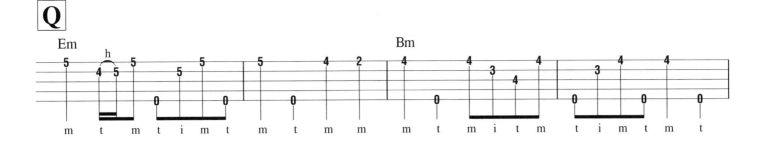

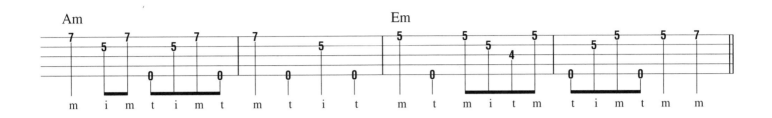

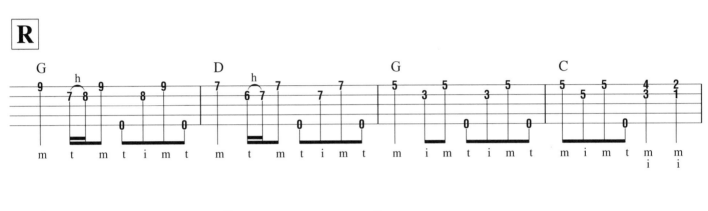

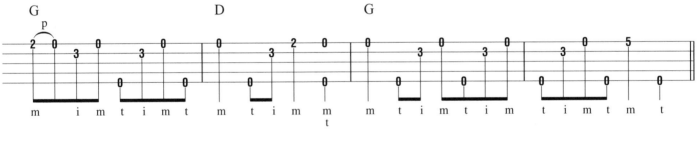

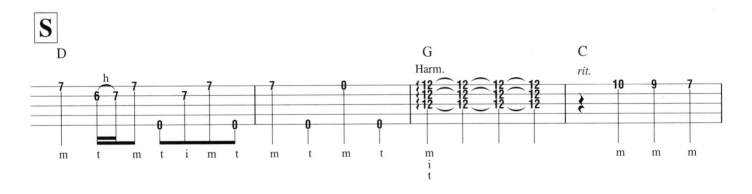

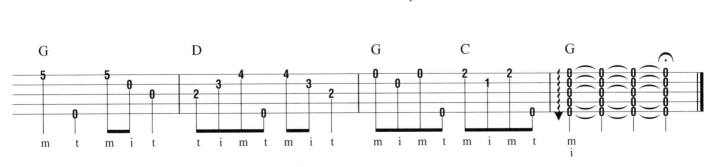

O Little Town of Bethlehem

Words by Phillips Brooks
Music by Lewis H. Redner

G tuning:
(5th-1st) G-D-G-B-D

Key of C

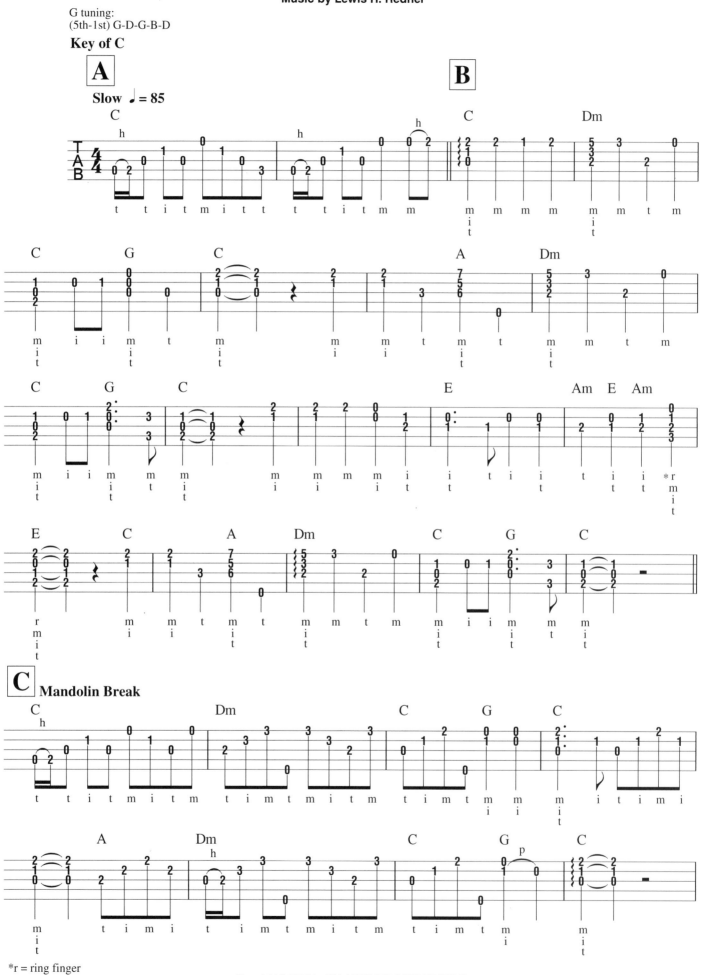

*r = ring finger

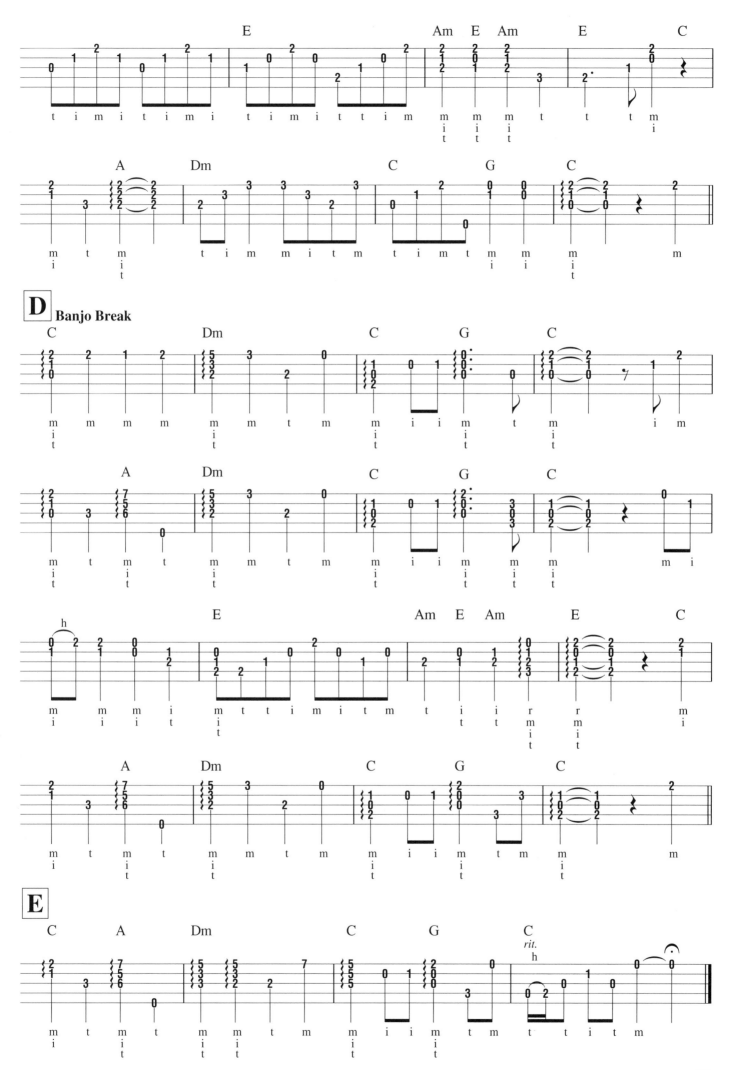

Silent Night

Words by Joseph Mohr
Translated by John F. Young
Music by Franz X. Gruber

G tuning:
(5th-1st) G-D-G-B-D

Key of D

Moderately ♩ = 108

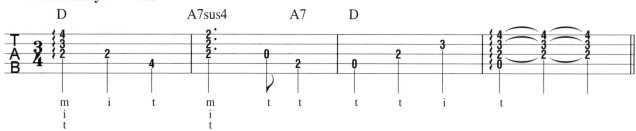

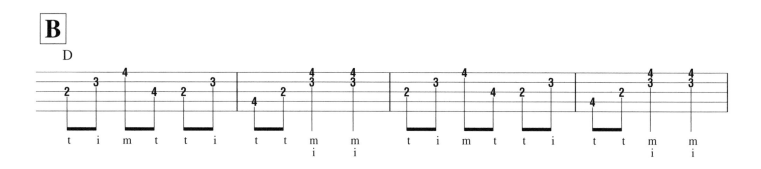

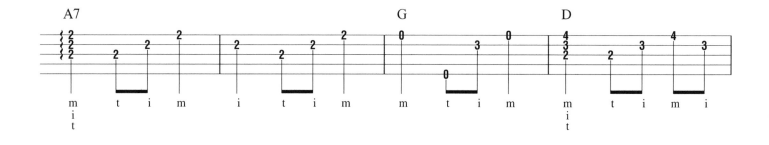

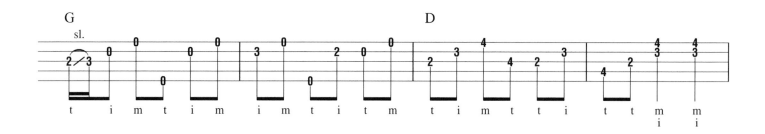

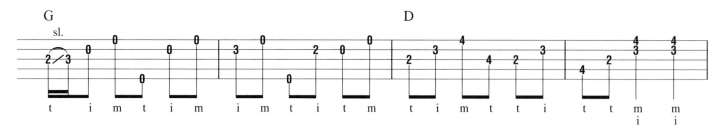

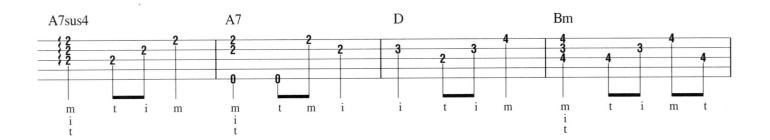

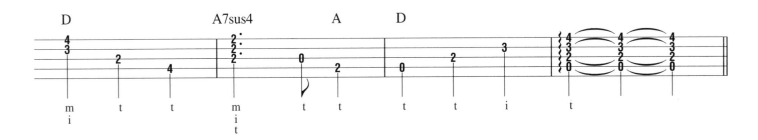

C Mandolin Break

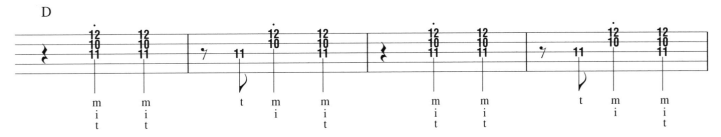

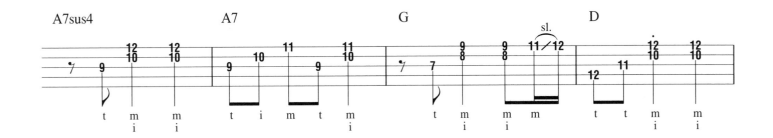

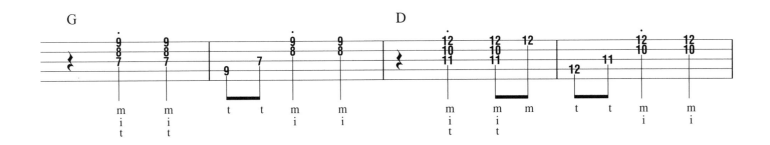

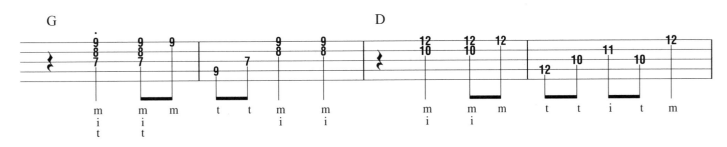

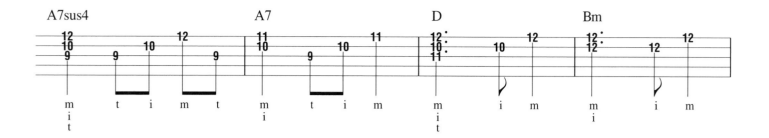

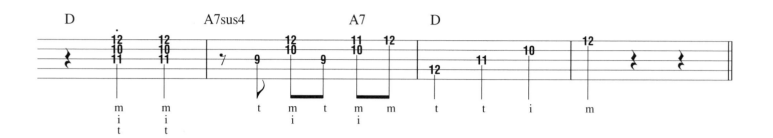

D Banjo Break

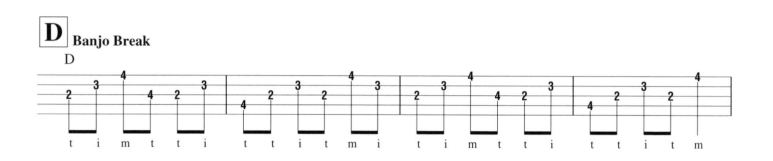

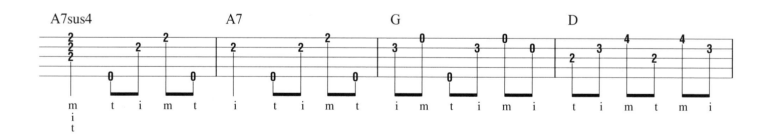

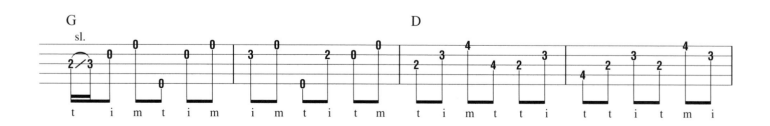

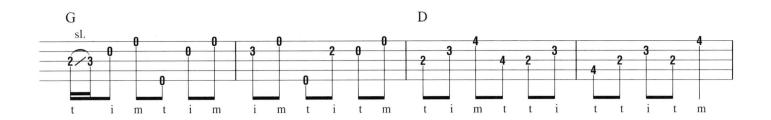

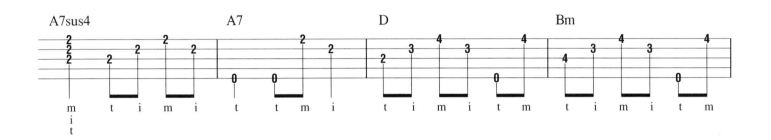

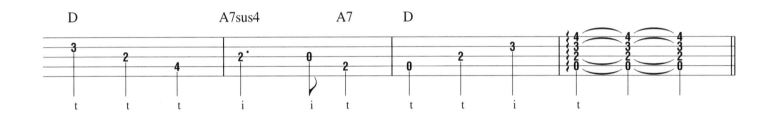

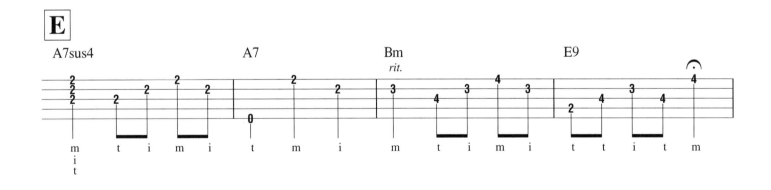

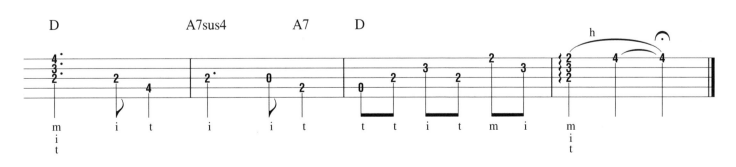

We Wish You a Merry Christmas

Traditional English Folksong

G tuning:
(5th-1st) G-D-G-B-D

Key of C

Fast ♩ = 152

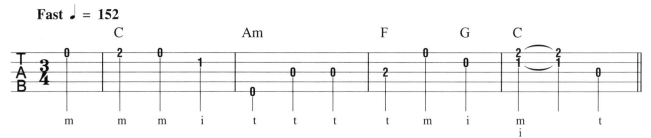

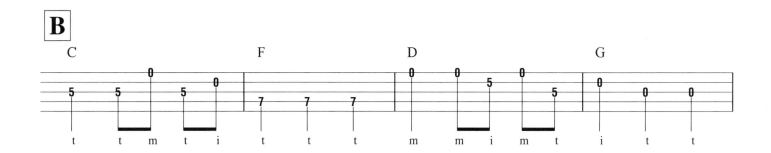

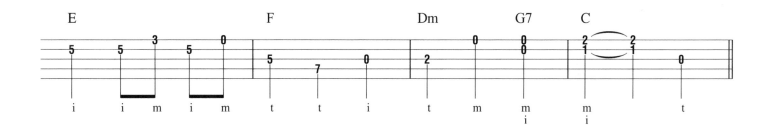

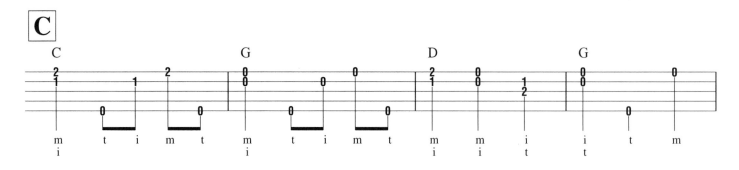

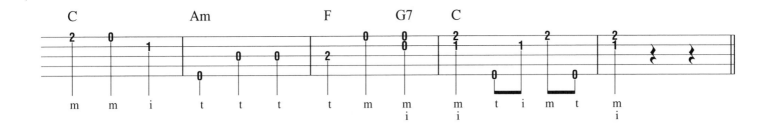

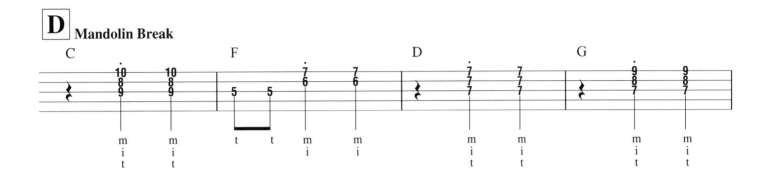

D Mandolin Break

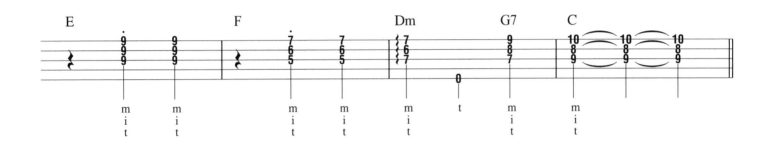

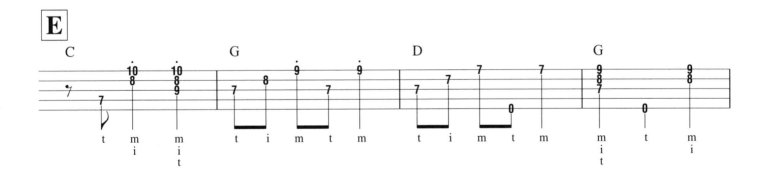

E

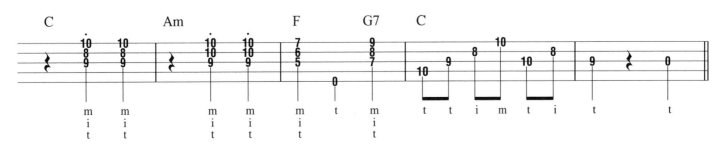

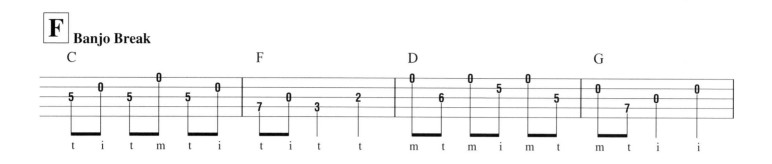

F Banjo Break

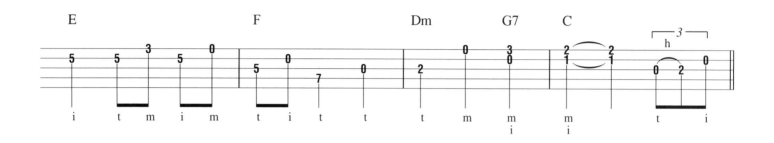

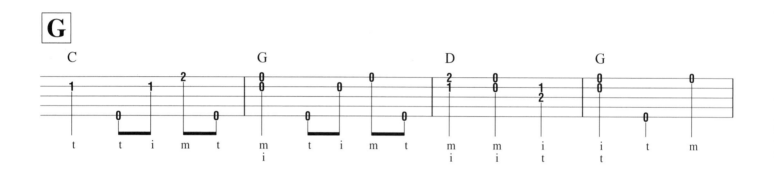

G

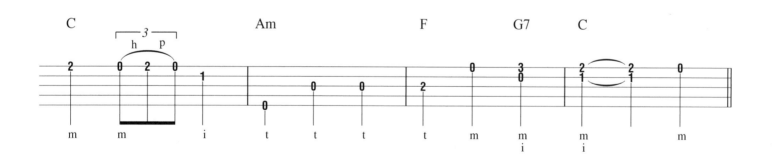

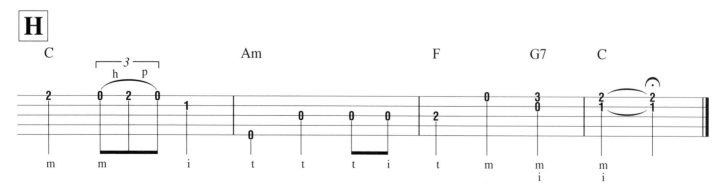

H